The Redemption of Scrooge

Leader Guide

# The Redemption of Scrooge

**The Redemption of Scrooge**
978-1-5018-2307-7
978-1-5018-2308-4 eBook

**The Redemption of Scrooge: Leader Guide**
978-1-5018-2309-1
978-1-5018-2310-7 eBook

**The Redemption of Scrooge: DVD**
978-1-5018-2311-4

**The Redemption of Scrooge: Youth Study Book**
978-1-5018-2316-9
978-1-5018-2317-6 eBook

**The Redemption of Scrooge: Worship Resources**
978-1-5018-2320-6 Flash Drive
978-1-5018-2321-3 Download

---

## Also by Matt Rawle

*The Faith of a Mockingbird*
*The Salvation of Doctor Who*
*Hollywood Jesus*

**For more information, visit MattRawle.com.**

# MATT RAWLE

# The Redemption of Scrooge

LEADER GUIDE
BY JOSH TINLEY

Abingdon Press / Nashville

**The Redemption of Scrooge**
Leader Guide

Copyright © 2016 Abingdon Press
All rights reserved.

This book is printed on elemental chlorine-free paper.

978-1-5018-2309-1

Scripture quotations unless noted otherwise are from the Common English Bible. Copyright © 2011 by the Common English Bible. All rights reserved. Used by permission. www.CommonEnglishBible.com.

Scripture quotation marked NIV is taken from the Holy Bible, New International Version®, NIV®. Copyright © 1973, 1978, 1984, 2011 by Biblica, Inc.™ Used by permission of Zondervan. All rights reserved worldwide. www.zondervan.com. The "NIV" and "New International Version" are trademarks registered in the United States Patent and Trademark Office by Biblica, Inc.™

Scripture quotations marked NRSV are taken from the New Revised Standard Version of the Bible, copyright 1989, Division of Christian Education of the National Council of the Churches of Christ in the United States of America. Used by permission. All rights reserved.

Quotations from *A Christmas Carol* are from Charles Dickens, *A Christmas Carol in Prose; Being A Ghost Story of Christmas* (London: Chapman and Hall, 1847), Kindle edition.

Quotations from *The Redemption of Scrooge* are from Matt Rawle, *The Redemption of Scrooge* (Nashville: Abingdon Press, 2016).

16 17 18 19 20 21 22 23 24 25—10 9 8 7 6 5 4 3 2 1
MANUFACTURED IN THE UNITED STATES OF AMERICA

# CONTENTS

# TO THE LEADER

Charles Dickens's classic novel *A Christmas Carol* is a story of brokenness and redemption. The beginning is dark—the book opens with, "Marley was dead." We soon meet Marley, former partner of the main character Ebenezer Scrooge, as a ghost. Marley's ghost promises Scrooge that a trio of ghosts will be visting him, and the reader is to presume that none of the visits will be pleasant. Scrooge begins the story as an unrepentant miser whose greed has caused harm to himself and others and ends with him a changed—a redeemed—man. Just as Christ brings light and hope to a world in darkness, the events of *A Christmas Carol* shine light into the darkness surrounding Scrooge's life, ultimately leading him to embrace the peace, hope, love, and joy we associate with Christmas.

In *The Redemption of Scrooge,* author and pastor Matt Rawle examines Dickens's classic novel, making connections between the story of Ebenezer Scrooge and the story that Christians tell during Advent and Christmas. His study looks at the four main parts of *A Christmas Carol*: the opening and visit of Marley's ghost, the visit of the Ghost of Christmas Past, the visit of the Ghost of Christmas Present, and the visit of the Ghost of Christmas Yet to Come. He looks at how we can draw from the past, present, and future important truths about brokenness and redemption and the Advent themes of peace, hope, love, and joy.

*The Redemption of Scrooge,* an Advent study, is part of the Pop in Culture Bible study series, a collection of studies about faith and popular culture. Each study uses a work of pop culture as a way to examine questions and issues of the Christian faith. Studies consist of a book, DVD, and leader guide. Our hope and prayer is that the studies will open our eyes to the spiritual truths that exist all around us in books, movies, music, and television.

As we walk with Christ, we discover the divine all around us, and in turn, the world invites us into a deeper picture of its Creator. Through this lens of God's redemption story, we are invited to look at culture in a new and inviting way. We are invited to dive into the realms of literature, art, and entertainment to explore and discover how God is working in and through us and in the world around us to tell God's great story of redemption.

## HOW TO FACILITATE THIS STUDY

Participants in this study do not need to have read Charles Dickens's *A Christmas Carol.* Nor do they need to have seen any of the many adapttaions of the novel for stage and screen. That said, your group likely will get more out of this study if participants have some familiarity with the story. You may encourage those in your group to prepare for the study by reading the novel or watching one of the movie adaptations.

This four-session Advent study makes use of the following components:

- the study book, *The Redemption of Scrooge* by Matt Rawle
- this Leader Guide
- *The Redemption of Scrooge* DVD

You will need a DVD player or computer and a television or projection screen so that you can watch the DVD segments as part of your group session. Participants in the study will need access to Bibles during the session; many activities will also require basic supplies including a markerboard or large sheets of paper and markers, pens and pencils, and index cards and/or slips of paper.

Each session is structured into a 60-minute format:

- Opening activity and prayer (5 minutes)
- Watch DVD segment (10 minutes)
- Study and discussion (35-40 minutes)
- Closing activity and prayer (5 minutes)

If you have more time in your session, or want to use more activities during your session, "Additional Options for Study and Discussion" are included for each chapter, listed after the closing prayer.

## HELPFUL HINTS

### Preparing for Each Session

- Pray for wisdom and discernment from the Holy Spirit, for you and for each member of the group, as you prepare for the study.
- Before each session, familiarize yourself with the content. Read the study book chapter again.
- Choose the session elements you will use during the group session, including the specific discussion questions you plan to cover. Be prepared, however, to adjust the

session as group members interact and as questions arise. Prepare carefully, but allow space for the Holy Spirit to move in and through the group members and through you as facilitator.

- Prepare the space where the group will meet so that the space will enhance the learning process. Ideally, group members should be seated around a table or in a circle so that all can see one another. Movable chairs are best so that the group easily can form pairs or small teams for discussion.

## Shaping the Learning Environment

- Create a climate of openness, encouraging group members to participate as they feel comfortable.
- Remember that some people will jump right in with answers and comments, while others need time to process what is being discussed.
- If you notice that some group members seem never to be able to enter the conversation, ask them if they have thoughts to share. Give everyone a chance to talk, but keep the conversation moving. Moderate to prevent a few individuals from doing all the talking.
- Communicate the importance of group discussions and group exercises.
- If no one answers at first during discussions, do not be afraid of silence. Count silently to ten, then say something such as, "Would anyone like to go first?" If no one responds, venture an answer yourself and ask for comments.
- Model openness as you share with the group. Group members will follow your example. If you limit your sharing to a surface level, others will follow suit.

- Encourage multiple answers or responses before moving on to the next question.
- Ask: "Why?" or "Why do you believe that?" or "Can you say more about that?" to help continue a discussion and give it greater depth.
- Affirm others' responses with comments such as "Great" or "Thanks" or "Good insight"—especially if it's the first time someone has spoken during the group session.
- Monitor your own contributions. If you are doing most of the talking, back off so that you do not train the group to listen rather than speak up.
- Remember that you do not have all the answers. Your job is to keep the discussion going and encourage participation.

## Managing the Session

- Honor the time schedule. If a session is running longer than expected, get consensus from the group before continuing beyond the agreed-upon ending time.
- Involve group members in various aspects of the group session, such as saying prayers or reading the Scripture.
- Note that the session guides sometimes call for breaking into smaller groups or pairs. This gives everyone a chance to speak and participate fully. Mix up the groups; don't let the same people pair up for every activity.
- As always in discussions that may involve personal sharing, confidentiality is essential. Group members should never pass along stories that have been shared in the group. Remind the group members at each session: confidentiality is crucial to the success of this study.

# Bah! Humbug!

## Planning the Session

### Session Goals

Through this session's discussion and activities, participants will be encouraged to:

- Familiarize themselves with *A Christmas Carol.*
- Examine how Advent is a season in which past, present, and future come together. (During this season we recall the events leading up to Jesus' birth two thousand years ago; we anticipate the ways in which Christ enters our lives today; and we look forward to Christ's promised return.)
- Explore the tension and relationship between God's grace and personal accountability.

- Look at the role that hope plays during the Advent season—particularly the hope that we have amid darkness and despair.
- Reflect on the witness of our spiritual ancestors.

## Preparation

- Read Chapter 1, "Bah! Humbug!" in Matt Rawle's *The Redemption of Scrooge*.
- Read through this Leader Guide session in its entirety to familiarize yourself with the material being covered.
- Read and reflect on the following Scriptures:
  o Matthew 1:1-17
  o Matthew 20:1-16
  o Mark 1:1-13
  o Luke 1:1-38
  o Luke 1:46-55
  o John 1:1-18
  o Galatians 6:7
  o Colossians 2:13-14
- You will want to have your DVD player or computer ready to watch the video segment. You might also want to have a markerboard or large sheet of paper available for recording group members' ideas.
- Have a Bible, paper for taking notes, and a pen or pencil available for every participant.
- If you will be doing the activity, "Merry Gentlemen and Gentlewomen," under "Additional Options for Study and Discussion," try to have a few hymnals or songbooks available that contain the hymn "God Rest You Merry, Gentlemen."

## GETTING STARTED

### Opening Activity and Prayer (5 minutes)

Begin by gauging your group's familiarity with Charles Dickens's novel *A Christmas Carol.*

- First, ask members of the group who've read the novel, *A Christmas Carol,* to stand (or raise their hands).
- While the novel readers remain standing, ask those who have seen a film or stage version of Dickens's *A Christmas Carol* to stand.
- Next, ask those who have seen a popular Hollywood take on the story, such as *Scrooged* or *A Muppet Christmas Carol,* to stand.
- Then, ask those to stand who—despite not having read the book or seen a movie adaptation—understand that there exists a story called *A Christmas Carol* about an old miser who has some run-ins with ghosts.
- Finally, ask those to stand who are familiar with the name "Scrooge" and associate that name with someone who is grumpy and cynical about Christmas.

If there are members of your group who have very limited knowledge of the story, give a brief summary (or read "A Quick Refresher," found at the beginning of *The Redemption of Scrooge*). Then discuss:

- How have you seen the name or image of Scrooge used in popular culture and advertising?
- Why do you think *A Christmas Carol* and the story of Ebenezer Scrooge resonates so much with our culture? Why do so many people relate to this story?

*God of our past, present, and future, bless our time together over the next few weeks. Guide us as we draw inspiration from a great work of literature during this time of preparation when we anticipate all the ways you have, do, and will enter our world. May we benefit from the wisdom of your people and your word. In Jesus' name. Amen.*

## LEARNING TOGETHER

### Watch DVD Segment (10 minutes)

### Study and Discussion of Book and DVD (35–40 minutes)

#### The Advent Time Warp

*Read aloud or summarize for the group:*

In *A Christmas Carol*, Ebenezer Scrooge is visited by three ghosts—the Ghosts of Christmas Past, Present, and Yet to Come. This idea of three ghosts is appropriate for the Christian season of Advent, which also brings together the past, present, and future.

Divide a markerboard or large sheet of paper into three columns, labeled "Past," "Present," and "Future."

Ask participants to brainstorm ways that Advent connects us with the past. List their ideas in the "Past" column on the markerboard or paper. Examples would include:

- During Advent, we remember the events leading up to Jesus' birth two millennia ago.
- We also look back further, to the ways in which God's people anticipated the coming of a Messiah.

- Advent also brings to mind the more recent past, such as memories from one's childhood or memories of loved ones who have died or moved away.

Then have participants brainstorm ways that Advent connects us to the present. List these ideas in the "Present" column. Examples would include:

- We actively participate in Advent through the ways we worship, the music we listen to, and the ways we decorate our homes and churches.
- Advent is an occasion to turn our hearts and minds toward Christ amid the busyness of Christmas shopping, work, exams (for those who are students or who have children who are), and other responsibilities.

Finally, ask participants to brainstorm ways that Advent connects us to the future. List these ideas in the "Future" column. Examples would include:

- Advent is a season of preparation. Most immediately, we prepare for our Christmas celebration.
- Advent looks ahead to Christ's return.
- During the Advent season, we often create memories that we will keep with us for many years.

Once you have a good list in all three columns, explain that Advent is a season that brings together the past, present, and future. Be sure to emphasize the following:

- Advent is the season when we remember the events leading up to Jesus' birth and prepare to celebrate Christmas.
- Advent is a season when we are especially mindful of how Jesus is present in our world today and when we prepare to encounter Jesus in our lives.

- Advent is the season when we look ahead to Jesus' promised return.

*Read aloud or summarize for the group:*

As Rawle writes, Advent helps us remember that, "Jesus came to save us from counting our past as our only reality.... Advent is like living in the wilderness between what was and what will be. Living into this tension, remembering God's promises, and depending on faith become spiritual disciplines that keep us from becoming Scrooges ourselves. Even though the Promised Land may seem far off, we hold tightly to the promises of our God, for 'he who promised is faithful' (Hebrews 10:23 NIV)" (*The Redemption of Scrooge*, pages 23-24).

## Just Deserts

Read aloud Galatians 6:7—if possible from a variety of translations. Ask:

- What do you think this verse means by, "A person will harvest what they plant" (CEB) or "You reap whatever you sow." (NRSV)?
- How might this verse be used to justify someone's misfortune (or taking delight in someone's misfortune)?

*Read aloud or summarize for the group:*

Ebenezer Scrooge takes a view of life that corresponds with this verse. Rawle says in the DVD segment that Scrooge lives according to Galatians 6:7 taken to the extreme. Because Scrooge feels as though every person is deserving of his or her circumstances (whether for good or for bad), he has little sympathy for those who struggle.

For discussion:

- How does this idea—that people reap what they sow—affect your attitudes toward other people?
- How might this verse alone be insufficient for understanding God's grace and judgment?

In order to get a broader view of God's grace and judgment, read aloud Colossians 2:13-14. Ask:

- What do these verses tell us about how God responds to the mistakes we make?
- How do these verses contradict or give new meaning to the idea that people get what they deserve?

For even more perspective, read Matthew 20:1-16. Discuss:

- How does this Scripture add to the discussion?
- What does Rawle say about this parable in the DVD segment?
- Would you say that the workers in this Scripture got what they deserved? Why, or why not?
- How does God's understanding of what we deserve differ from our understanding? What does this parable tell us about God's grace?
- Rawle, in the DVD segment, says that God's economy doesn't follow the same rules as the world. What does this parable tell us about God's economy? How do the "rules" in this parable differ from the economic rules of the culture in which we live?
- Considering all of these Scriptures together, how should we understand Galatians 6:7?

**Magnify the Lord**

*Read aloud or summarize for the group:*

When Jesus' mother, Mary, learned that she would be giving birth to the Messiah, she broke into song.

- Read aloud Mary's song from Luke 1:46-55. This song is traditionally known as the *Magnificat*. *Magnificat* is the Latin translation of the song's opening phrase, "My soul magnifies the Lord" (Luke 1:46 NRSV). Ask:
    o What does Mary's song tell us about God and God's priorities?
    o How does Mary's view of the world contrast with Ebenezer Scrooge's?

Divide participants into groups of three or four. Ask each group to write its own version of Mary's *Magnificat* using language and examples better suited to a current-day audience. If groups are musically inclined, encourage them to put their songs to a tune.

After all the groups have had time to work, invite each group to present its song. Then ask:

- Which Advent and Christmas songs have themes similar to Mary's song?
- How can the church better honor the themes and ideas in Mary's song during the Advent season?
- How are you "highly favored"? In what ways has God "done great things" for you (Luke 1:48-49)?
- How can you use your blessings to participate in God's work of lifting "up the lowly" (Luke 1:52)?

## WRAPPING UP

**Closing Activity: Your Marley's Ghost (5 minutes)**

Read aloud Hebrews 12:1-2. Ask:

- To whom do you think the author is referring with the phrase, "great cloud of witnesses"?

*Read aloud or summarize for the group:*

Prior to these verses, the Book of Hebrews had run through a list of heroes of the faith, including several great Israelite prophets and leaders.

The first ghost to visit Ebenezer Scrooge in *A Christmas Carol* was the ghost of Scrooge's old partner, Jacob Marley. Like Scrooge, Marley had been a miser. Only after his death had Marley come to terms with errors he'd made while he was alive. Though most of us would prefer not to be visited by ghosts, we all know people who have gone before us who could impart valuable advice to us.

- Challenge members of the group to think of one person who is no longer living who might be able to offer them valuable wisdom and guidance. They need not think of someone who, like Marley, regrets how he or she lived—someone whose wisdom comes from realizing his or her mistakes. They also need not select someone with whom they worked closely.
- Once participants have selected a person, have them write about what wisdom that person might impart to them. Give everyone a few minutes to work, then, if your group is large, have participants pair off or form groups of three. Invite the groups to talk about who they selected and the advice they'd expect to receive.

Come back together and discuss:

- What is one thing you learned about God, Scripture, or the church during this session?
- What is one thing you learned from your fellow participants that you will take with you this Advent season?

**Closing Prayer**

*God of Advent and Christmas, thank you for entering our world as a child many years ago; thank you for entering our lives today; and thank you for the hope of your promised return. As we travel through this Advent season, let us be mindful of your presence and your will. Empower us to bring the hope of Christ to all of your people. We pray all these things in the name of Christ, who is past, present, and future. Amen.*

# ADDITIONAL OPTIONS FOR STUDY AND DISCUSSION

**Marley Was Dead (15-20 minutes)**

*Read aloud or summarize for the group:*

*A Christmas Carol* begins ominously with, "Marley was dead." In *The Redemption of Scrooge*, Rawle writes, "Dickens wants us to know this important fact...right from the very beginning. This statement sets the tone for the story and foreshadows what's to come" (page 21). Ask:

- If you had no familiarity with *A Christmas Carol* and read that opening line, what might you expect from the story?

Often an opening line, paragraph, or scene sets the tone for the rest of a story. With this in mind, take a look at how each of the four Gospels begins.

- Depending on your available time and the number of people in your group, go over the openings of the Gospels as a group, or divide participants into four teams and assign each team one of the following Gospel passages:
  o Matthew 1:1-17
  o Mark 1:1-13
  o Luke 1:1-38
  o John 1:1-18

- For each of the four Gospel openings, discuss:
  o Based on these verses alone, what tone, do you think, is the author setting for this Gospel?
  o Again, based on these verses alone, what would you expect this Gospel to say about Jesus?
  o What did you learn about the beginnings of the four Gospels that you didn't know prior to this activity?
  o How does the tone set by the opening of each of the Gospels compare to the tone set by the opening of *A Christmas Carol*?
  o How is the tone of a story essential to conveying the truths or lessons it wants to impart?

**Advent or Christmas? (10-15 minutes)**

*Read aloud or summarize for the group:*

Dickens titled his novel *A Christmas Carol*, even though it's a book and not a song. Rawle writes that Dickens's *Carol* was "certainly intended to invoke a reader's familiarity with

Christmas songs since the story is organized into five staves, or stanzas, like a piece of music without musical notes" (*The Redemption of Scrooge,* page 25).

Few things connect us to the Advent and Christmas seasons more than hymns, carols, and popular songs. While we often lump these songs together under the category "Christmas music," some hymns and songs are more appropriate during Advent, while others are a better fit for the Christmas season. Though we often treat Advent as pre-Christmas, Advent and Christmas are distinct seasons. Advent is a season of hopeful preparation when we anticipate Christ entering our world. Christmas is a season when we celebrate Jesus' birth and the good news that God came to live among us in human form.

- Make a list, on a markerboard or large sheet of paper, of hymns and songs that you associate with Christmas. Focus on songs that are about Christ (rather than about Santa Claus, snow, or other seasonal elements). Once you have between twenty and thirty hymns and songs, challenge participants to sort them into two categories: Advent and Christmas.

- As much as possible, come to a group consensus before putting a song in one category or the other. If your group is especially large, divide participants into smaller teams and have each team sort the songs. When there is dispute about where a song should go, have participants make a case for one category or the other.

Then discuss:

- Do you think of Advent and Christmas as two distinct seasons or as one time of year?
- Why do you think the has church traditionally separated Advent and Christmas into two seasons?

- What is the value of setting aside a time of year for hopeful preparation (Advent) and a time for joyous celebration (Christmas)? How can observing these separate seasons help us focus on and develop different aspects of our faith and relationship with God?
- Based on your knowledge of *A Christmas Carol*, in what ways is it an Advent story? How is it a Christmas story?

**Merry Gentlemen and Gentlewomen (10 minutes)**

Distribute hymnals or songbooks that include the popular Christmas song, "God Rest You Merry, Gentlemen."

Ask:

- How familiar are you with this song and its lyrics?
- How much thought have you given to what the song's lyrics mean?

Have participants open hymnals or songbooks to "God Rest You Merry, Gentlemen," a song Dickens mentions specifically in *A Christmas Carol.* Give them a few minutes to read the words and reflect on their meaning. Suggest that they think about:

- To whom does title refer?
- What is the song saying to these "merry gentlemen"?

Discuss the meaning of the lyrics and participants' answers to these questions. Then ask:

- Read what Rawle says about this song in *The Redemption of Scrooge* on pages 30-34. What does he say about how the meaning of the song may have changed based on punctuation?

- Based on your understanding of the lyrics, and what Rawle writes about Scrooge's nephew in *The Redemption of Scrooge*, "God Rest You Merry, Gentlemen or God Rest You, Merry Gentlemen," how does Fred, Scrooge's nephew in *A Christmas Carol*, embody the song's meaning?
- How can you embody the spirit of this song during the Advent and Christmas season?

Rawle says about "God Rest You Merry, Gentlemen, "The words are hopeful.... Yet the music is composed in a minor key, giving it a somber tone" (*The Redemption of Scrooge*, page 33).

Discuss:

- What is the relationship between hope and despair? Why might it be appropriate to set hopeful lyrics to a somber tune?
- How does the idea of hope amid darkness apply to the Advent season?

## Session 2

# THE REMEMBRANCE OF CHRISTMAS PAST

### PLANNING THE SESSION

#### Session Goals

Through this session's discussion and activities, participants will be encouraged to:

- Reflect on past Advent and Christmas celebrations and why certain memories stick with us.
- Learn about Jesus' humanity and vulnerability and the significance of God coming to live on earth in the form of a small child.
- Explore the importance of knowing who we are as followers of Christ and being able to tell our story.

- Consider how our senses draw us closer to God and how we engage the senses during worship.
- Learn the significance of the Advent wreath and each of the Advent candles.

## Preparation

- Read Chapter 2, "The Remembrance of Christmas Past," in Matt Rawle's *The Redemption of Scrooge.*
- Read through this Leader Guide session in its entirety to familiarize yourself with the material being covered.
- Read and reflect on the following Scriptures:
  o Matthew 2:13-23
  o Luke 16:19-31
  o Galatians 1:13-24
- You will want to have your DVD player or computer ready to watch the video segment. You might also want to have a markerboard or large sheet of paper available for recording group members' ideas.
- Have a Bible, paper for taking notes, and a pen or pencil available for every participant.
- Have blank paper and colored pencils, markers, or crayons available for the activities "Christmas Past" and "A Story in Candles."

## GETTING STARTED

### Opening Activity and Prayer (5 minutes)

Ask participants to think of their earliest Christmas memories. Invite each person to describe his or her memory and discuss:

- What, if anything, is special or significant about these early memories? Why do you think you are able to retain them after so many years?

28

- Do you think these earliest memories say anything about your priorities or who you are? If so, what do they say?
- Why are memories important? What can we learn from them?

*God of the past, bless our time together as we reflect on our memories and on the wisdom of those who came before us. As we tell our stories, let us be mindful of how our stories are part of your story and open our minds so that we may learn from others' stories. In the name of Christ, who came to us in the past as a baby in Bethlehem. Amen.*

## LEARNING TOGETHER

### Watch DVD Segment (10 minutes)

### Study and Discussion of Book and DVD (35–40 minutes)

#### Christmas Past

Give each participant a sheet of paper and set out pens and pencils and colored pencils, crayons, or markers. Invite each person to spend a few minutes illustrating, through drawing or writing, his or her "Christmas past." What traditions, people, places, and symbols epitomize their Christmases when they were younger or growing up? Participants may focus on a particular Christmas or Christmases from a particular time in their lives, or they may combine elements from various Christmases they remember.

Allow everyone several minutes to work, then invite volunteers to present their illustrations. (Alternatively, participants could separate into pairs or groups of three and share their work with one another, if your group is large.) Then discuss:

- What parts of your past Christmases are most meaningful to you?
- How has your celebration of Christmas changed throughout your life? How has the meaning of the holiday changed for you?
- How has Christ influenced your past Christmas celebrations?

**Your Story (in Fewer Than One Hundred Words)**

*Read aloud or summarize for the group:*

Matt Rawle, in *The Redemption of Scrooge,* discusses how Ebenezer Scrooge had forgotten his own story. He'd lost sight of the memories that had shaped him when he was younger. When the Ghost of Christmas Past showed Scrooge events from his childhood, Scrooge was able to piece his story back together and reclaim some of the identity he'd lost.

- Read Galatians 1:13-24, in which the Apostle Paul tells his story to the church in Galatia. Discuss:
  o According to Paul, what are the important parts of his story?
  o How did these parts of his story shape who he became as a follower of Christ and leader of the church?

It's important that we know our stories, that we remember who we are and what we've been through. With that in mind, challenge participants to write their life's story in one hundred words or fewer. They obviously won't be able to cover every detail, so they'll have to choose what facts and events have done the most to shape who they are.

Allow five or so minutes for everyone to write (and edit) their stories. Then ask if any participants are willing to read aloud their hundred-word life stories. Afterward, ask:

- How difficult was it to condense your life into fewer than one hundred words?
- How does your story affect how you live and the decisions you make?
- On the whole, what memories would you say stick with you the most, good memories or bad memories?
- Why is it important to remember the negative parts of our story? (Hint: Jesus came to redeem us, even those parts of our pasts that are painful.)

## A Glimpse of Redemption

*Read aloud or summarize for the group:*

The story we profess as Christians is a story of redemption. God creates; sin makes a mess of God's creation; then God goes to great lengths to clean up the mess and mend the brokenness. We see this in the stories of individuals, in the story of God's people, and in the story of all creation.

Ask participants to brainstorm people or groups from history or from the news who are known for having been redeemed. If they struggle to come up with examples, start with biblical figures such as Paul, Moses, David, and the woman at the well in John 4.

Once you have a good list, ask:

- What can we learn from these examples about God's work of redemption?

*Read aloud or summarize for the group:*

While Christmas for many is a time of joy, for many others it is a difficult time—a time of sadness and brokenness. Rawle says, in the DVD segment, that whether Christmas is a happy time for you, or whether Christmas brings with it difficult memories, God is with you. We can find comfort and joy in the truth that our God is a God of redemption. And we can extend this comfort and joy to those who most need to hear the truth of redemption during the Advent and Christmas seasons.

For discussion:

- How should our understanding and experience of God's redemption affect our attitudes toward other people?
- How can you bring the hope of God's redemption to those who need it most?

## WRAPPING UP

### Closing Activity: Your Ghost of Christmas Past (5 minutes)

*Read aloud or summarize for the group:*

In *A Christmas Carol* the Ghost of Christmas Past visits Scrooge to teach him lessons about who he is and who he has become. Throughout this session, you have revisited your past. You have recounted your earliest memories; you have described your "Christmas past"; and you have told the story of your life. Now imagine that the Ghost of Christmas Past has come to visit you.

If your group is large, divide into pairs or teams of three to discuss the following questions:

- Of the memories you have recalled today—or other memories that you haven't—which memories do you think the Ghost of Christmas past might show you? (These need not be Christmas memories only.) Why? Would these memories be positive, negative, or a combination of the two?

- What lessons, do you think, would the ghost expect you to learn from these memories? Specifically, what might the ghost expect you to learn from your positive memories? What might the ghost expect you to learn from the negative ones?

Invite volunteers to share some of their answers to these questions. Then discuss:

- What have you learned about yourself and about your faith during this session—particularly through reflecting on your memories of the past?
- What have you learned from Scrooge's encounter with the Ghost of Christmas Past and from some of the Scriptures we studied as a part of this session?
- How might setting aside time to reflect on your past— both in terms of your personal story and of the larger story of God's people—be a valuable spiritual practice?
- What dangers might arise by spending too much time dwelling on the past and on memories? How can you avoid these pitfalls while still benefiting from lessons and wisdom from the past?

## Closing Prayer

*God of Christmases past, you have been at work in our lives since the beginning. Open our eyes to all of the ways you have been at work in our memories and in the Advent and Christmas traditions that have been handed down to us.*

*Give us the courage to examine mistakes we've made in the
past so that we will continue to grow into the people you
created us to be. In Jesus' name. Amen.*

## ADDITIONAL OPTIONS FOR
## STUDY AND DISCUSSION

### The Chasm (10 minutes)

Read aloud Luke 16:19-31. Discuss:

- In this parable, a chasm or crevasse separates the wealthy
  man from Lazarus after the two men have died. What
  chasm separated these two men while they were alive?
- What chasms separate you from people in your community, or elsewhere in the world, who have significant
  needs? (Examples might include apathy, ignorance,
  distance, cultural differences, and so on.)

Explain that, in *A Christmas Carol,* Ebenezer Scrooge finds
himself on the wrong side of a similar chasm. He witnesses a
joyful scene from his childhood in his hometown, but he cannot
join in the celebration. Ask:

- What chasms have kept you from being able to celebrate
  with others? (Possibilities include a grudge, prejudice,
  envy, grief, economic disadvantages, and so on.)
- Which of these chasms were beyond your control? Which
  were of your own doing?
- Which of these chasms were you able to bridge? Which, if
  any, still separate you from the joy of others?
- What can you do to bridge these chasms that still exist in
  your life?

## A Story in Candles (15 minutes)

Ask participants who have seen *Disney's A Christmas Carol* how the Ghost of Christmas Past appears in this movie. (Answer: He appears as a candle.) Then ask:

- What roles do candles play in our Advent and Christmas celebrations?

Hand out paper and set out markers, crayons, or colored pencils. Ask participants to make a sketch of an Advent wreath with its candles. Tell them to create this drawing from memory, without looking up images on their phones or other devices.

After they've had a minute or so to work, have participants show their work. Make note of any significant differences between the participants' drawings. Then discuss their wreaths using the following questions:

- How many candles are on your wreath? (An Advent wreath should include four candles, one for each Sunday of Advent. Be aware that the sequence of the candles varies from tradition to tradition, but usually not the names of the candles.)
- What colors are the candles? (Traditionally Advent candles have been purple, the liturgical color for seasons of preparation. In recent years many churches have switched to blue to distinguish Advent from Lent. Blue is a color of hope. On the third Sunday, some churches celebrate "Joy Sunday" or "Gaudete Sunday." The candle for that Sunday may be rose colored because that color represents joy.)
- What else does your wreath include?

Challenge participants to come up with, from memory, what each of the four Advent candles represents. If you have liturgically minded participants who already know, have them withhold their answers for few moments. (If you have a large number of participants, have them guess the meanings of the candles in groups of three or four.)

After they've had a few minutes to guess, go over the answers, and then reveal each candle's meaning. Talk about how the theme of the candle is important to the Advent and Christmas season.

- **Peace:** Because we are people of hope we strive for peace, even in a world of violence and brokenness.
- **Hope:** We live in a time between Christ's resurrection and Christ's return when we look forward hopefully to God making all things new.
- **Love:** Love is the very nature of God.
- **Joy:** Christ brought joy to a world that needed it badly.

After you've gone over the meaning of the candles, ask:

- How do symbols and rituals such as lighting the Advent candles affect or enhance your worship of God during the Advent and Christmas seasons?
- Does knowing the meaning of the candles change how you experience them?
- How do the Advent candles tell the story of who we are and what we believe as Christians? (How are peace, hope, love, and joy a part of the story we tell during Advent? How are they a part of God's story of creation and redemption?)

**A Season of Senses (15 minutes)**

Ask:

- When does Christmas start to "feel" like Christmas for you?

36

Divide a markerboard or large sheet of paper into five columns or sections, one for each of the five traditional senses. Label the sections, "Smells," "Tastes," "Sounds," "Sights," and "Textures." Go through each section and ask participants to brainstorm items for that sense that they associate with the Advent and Christmas seasons. (If you have limited time and a large number of participants, divide participants into five teams and have each team handle one of the senses.)

After you have a good list for each sense, discuss:

- Which of these smells, tastes, sounds, sights, and textures do you associate most strongly with the Advent and Christmas seasons?

Historically, Christian worship has engaged the senses, perhaps especially during special seasons. Ask:

- How do we, as a church, engage the senses during the Advent and Christmas seasons?
- What sights, sounds, smells, tastes, and textures are important parts of our Advent and Christmas worship experiences?

The miracle of Christmas is that, in Jesus, God took on flesh. God became a human being with human senses who people could see and hear and touch. Ask:

- What is the significance of God taking on human form, particularly the form of a baby, instead of coming to earth in some other manner?
- What seasonal sights, sounds, tastes, textures, and smells remind you of Jesus' humanity and vulnerability?

## Session 3

# THE LIFE OF CHRISTMAS PRESENT

## PLANNING THE SESSION

### Session Goals

Through this session's discussion and activities, participants will be encouraged to:

- Think critically about wants and needs and how we could more faithfully use the resources God has entrusted to us.
- Consider the significance of God revealing the good news of Jesus' birth first to shepherds.
- Be aware and thankful of the ways in which God has blessed us and the ways in which God is blessing us.

- Examine the roles we have to play in the work God is doing in the world right now.

## Preparation

- Read Chapter 3, "The Life of Christmas Present," in Matt Rawle's *The Redemption of Scrooge.*
- Read through this Leader Guide session in its entirety to familiarize yourself with the material being covered.
- Read and reflect on the following Scriptures:
  o Exodus 16:13-21
  o Matthew 20:1-16
  o Luke 2:1-10
  o Luke 15:1-10
- You will want to have your DVD player or computer ready to watch the video segment. You might also want to have a markerboard or large sheet of paper available for recording group members' ideas.
- Have a Bible, paper for taking notes, and a pen or pencil available for every participant.
- If you are doing the activity "God Bless Us, Every One" under "Additional Options for Study and Discussion," you may want to have available hymnals or songbooks containing "Hark! the Herald Angels Sing."

# GETTING STARTED

## Opening Activity and Prayer (5 minutes)

As participants arrive, open your time together and get in the holiday spirit by discussing the following questions:

- What does your "Christmas present" as in this year, look like? What traditions, people, places, and symbols epitomize Christmas for you, at this point in your life?
- What parts of your "Christmas present" carry over from Christmases past?
- How has Christmas changed for you as you've grown older? What new elements have you added to your Christmas celebrations?
- How does Christ factor into your present celebrations?

*God of today, bless our time together as we discuss how you are at work in the here and now. As we consider how you are at work in our world today and in our Advent and Christmas celebrations, let us be mindful of your will and of what you call us to do and be. In the name of the Holy Spirit, who is present with us always. Amen.*

## LEARNING TOGETHER

### Watch DVD Segment (10 minutes)

### Study and Discussion of
### Book and DVD (35–40 minutes)

#### Good News? Maybe for You

*Read aloud or summarize for the group:*

In *A Christmas Carol*, the Ghost of Christmas Present takes Ebenezer Scrooge through the town where he lives. Rawle writes of what Scrooge sees on this tour: "The houses look bleak, as the wintry weather seems to emphasize the chilly disposition of everything he sees. It is not that the streets were full of squalor; rather the grayness of it all left little room for good tidings and the usual cheerfulness we have come to know during the holiday season" (*The Redemption of Scrooge*, page 86). Despite this, there was still an air of happiness on the streets. Dickens wrote, in *A Christmas Carol*, "There was nothing very cheerful in the climate or the town, and yet was there an air of cheerfulness abroad that the clearest summer air and brightest summer sun might have endeavoured to diffuse in vain" (Stave Three).

Discuss:

- Are there areas of our city that strike you as bleak? How much time have you spent in these parts of the city?
- How have you seen hope and cheerfulness amid the bleakness in this part of town (or in another place you've visited)?

Read aloud the Christmas story in Luke 2:1-20. Discuss:

- What was bleak and difficult about the circumstances surrounding the first Christmas?
- How was hope and joy present despite this bleakness?

*Read aloud or summarize for the group:*

Christmas is very much about hope amid darkness, not only because of the circumstances in which Jesus was born, but also because we celebrate it during the coldest, darkest time of the year (at least in the Northern Hemisphere). For many the joy of Christmas is also muted by the busyness and stress that surrounds the season.

Rawle says, "Throughout Scripture, God's justice involves a lifting up of the lowly, not a divine mandate that all receive the same" (*The Redemption of Scrooge,* page 93). The Bible shows us that God provides for all people, even if God often doesn't work in ways we'd expect. It also shows us that God has a particular concern for those who are lost, poor, or in difficult circumstances.

Divide participants into three teams. Assign each team one of the following three Scriptures:

- Exodus 16:13-21
- Matthew 20:1-16
- Luke 15:1-10

Each team should read its Scripture passage and discuss the following questions:

- What does this Scripture say about how God provides?
- How are God's actions or words in this Scripture at odds with how human beings typically understand justice?
- What does this Scripture say about God lifting up the lowly?

Give teams about five minutes to read and discuss. Then invite each team to briefly summarize its scripture and answers to the questions above.

**"Never Such a Goose"**

*Read aloud or summarize for the group:*

The Ghost of Christmas Present takes Scrooge on a tour of several Christmas celebrations. Most notably, the ghost and Scrooge look in on Christmas dinner at the Cratchit house. Bob Cratchit is Ebenezer Scrooge's clerk, whom Scrooge underpays and treats with contempt. Dickens shows us the financially challenged Cratchit family at Christmas dinner, feasting on a goose that others might not consider very impressive: "There never was such a goose. Bob said he didn't believe there ever was such a goose cooked. Its tenderness and flavour, size and cheapness, were the themes of universal admiration" (*A Christmas Carol,* Stave Three).

In the DVD segment, Rawle points out that Bob Cratchit sees something different around his table than the rest of us. The family meal is neither abundant nor beautiful, but Bob still marvels, "Have you ever seen such a goose?" He sees something different, and if we take the time to look at the gospel story, we might see God's story that is lying just below the surface.

Discuss:

What does Rawle say about the story that lies just below the surface of the account of Jesus' birth and early life? (For example, Rawle specifically mentions the significance of Jesus being placed in a feeding trough.)

To understand and appreciate how God is at work among us, we have to adopt the attitude of Bob Cratchit and look beneath the surface of what seems to be going on in our lives. In this spirit, ask participants to identify a meal they've had recently that was filling and nourishing but that most people might not regard as a "nice" meal. (*Note*: "Nourishing" doesn't necessary mean healthy, just that the meal included some amount of protein, vitamins, and other nutrients. This might include a frozen dinner, a fast-food meal, or something prepared quickly from a can or box. While such a meal might not seem impressive, plenty of people who are hungry or experiencing food insecurity would consider it a blessing.)

Challenge participants to find aspects of the meal that are worthy of praise, such as the taste, the convenience, the nutritional value, the price, or the way it satisfied their hunger, and to write down their thoughts. Ask that they consider all the people involved in preparing the meal: those who cooked the food, those who delivered the food, those who packaged the food, those who harvested the ingredients, and so on.

Give participants a few minutes to work, then invite volunteers to read aloud what they have written. Discuss:

- Would you normally consider the meal you described a blessing? Why, or why not?
- What blessings in your life do you have a tendency to overlook?
- How much thought do you put into who is responsible for your meals, including the fast, cheap, and mundane meals?
- How might our attitudes and behaviors change when we take the time to be grateful for all that God has blessed us with, even those things that we take for granted?

Rawle writes, "It is easy to get distracted with the decorations, lights, and festive music of Christmas; but at its heart, the first Nativity is a story born out of poverty, where scarcity is transformed into abundance by a God who will stop at nothing to be with us" (*The Redemption of Scrooge*, page 97). Discuss:

- How is the Nativity story "born out of poverty"?
- The angels revealed the good news of Jesus' birth not to kings and lords but to shepherds. Why do you think God chose shepherds? What does this tell us about God and how God works? (*Note*: As needed, read the story of the first Christmas from Luke 2:1-20 for context.)

- How should the circumstances of the first Christmas influence our observance and celebration of current-day Christmas?
- How should the circumstances of the first Christmas influence our attitudes (particularly our attitudes toward other people) as we make our way through the rest of the year?

**Christmas in Action**

Divide participants into teams of four. Each group should discuss tangible ways that they can bring joy and hope to people who are experiencing darkness during the Advent and Christmas seasons. Groups can either decide on one act that they will perform together, as a team, or acts that each individual will perform based on his or her abilities and opportunities. It is important that any task they chose be specific, measurable (meaning that there is an objective way to know that it has been completed), and something they can do before your next meeting.

Have every person or group name aloud their task so that members of the group can hold one another accountable for completing them.

*Option*: Instead of having small teams or individuals commit to an activity, determine something that you can do as an entire group. This could be a project that you initiate or an existing effort that you all can participate in. Before you start something new, research active organizations and ministries in your congregation or community that already are addressing the need you've identified.

# Wrapping Up

## Closing: Your Ghost of Christmas Present (5 minutes)

*Read aloud or summarize for the group:*

In *A Christmas Carol,* the Ghost of Christmas Present wanted Scrooge to see how certain people in his life were observing the Christmas season. Scrooge sees people embracing the joy of the season, he sees a family of modest means appreciating the blessings they do have, and he sees the negative effects his actions are having on others.

Ask participants to imagine that the Ghost of Christmas Present visited them. What would the ghost want them to see and to learn? If you'd like, have participants illustrate in journaling or drawing what the Ghost of Christmas Present might show them. If your group is large, divide up into pairs or trios.

Give participants a few minutes to work, then invite willing participants to briefly show or describe what they drew.

Before you depart, if you'd like, remind participants of any commitments they made as a part of activities in this session. Encourage them to follow through on these before your next meeting.

## Closing Prayer

*God of the present, open our eyes to all the ways you are present in our world, particularly the ways you are at work through other people. Open our minds so that we can learn from those who embrace blessings that we take for granted. We pray these things in the name of your Holy Spirit, who is with us always. Amen.*

# ADDITIONAL OPTIONS FOR STUDY AND DISCUSSION

### Wants and Needs (10-15 minutes)

Challenge participants to list all of the purchases they've made in the past week (no matter how small). After they've put their lists together, ask them to separate these purchases into needs and wants. (One could make the case that needs only include those things absolutely necessary to survival, but allow participants to broaden the definition. For instance, a person can subsist without a new pair of work shoes, but there are nonetheless valid professional and arch-support-related reasons to buy shoes. Groceries would count as needs, even if they go above and beyond what is required to live, but meals out would go into the want category.) Ask:

- Do you think that the amount of money you spent this week on wants is similar to what you would spend in an average week?
- How difficult would it be for you to stop spending 50 percent of the money you're currently spending on wants? What about 75 percent? One hundred percent?
- If you were to eliminate half or more of your wants, what other things could you spend this money on?

If the group is too large for sharing together, have participants divide into pairs or groups of three. Pairs or groups should discuss their ideas for using their want money differently. This could involve donating the money to a worthy organization or investing it in something that would benefit the church, community, or family. Each person should set a goal for how they will make better use of their discretionary spending. If appropriate, encourage group mates to hold each other accountable for meeting those goals between now and your next session.

## I Can't Wait (5 minutes)

Ask:

- Christmas is a time of waiting and anticipation. What do you look forward to most during the Advent and Christmas seasons?
- What are we, as Christians, looking forward to during Advent?

*Read aloud or summarize for the group:*

In *A Christmas Carol* the Ghost of Christmas Present shows Scrooge that Tiny Tim is very ill and will likely die. Scrooge is horrified by the thought, especially because he realizes that his words and actions are partially responsible for Tim's deteriorating condition. God often works through human beings, and our words and behaviors can have a bigger impact than we'd ever imagine.

Though Advent is a time of waiting, God doesn't expect us to wait passively. God has work for us to do. Discuss:

- How have you seen God at work through human beings?
- What work might God have for you to do?
- What might happen if you fail to do these things? Who might be hurt?

## God Bless Us, Every One (10-20 minutes)

*Read aloud or summarize for the group:*

The phrase, "God bless Us, Every One," said by Bob Cratchit's son Tiny Tim, is one of the most famous lines in *A Christmas*

*Carol* (Stave Five) and, arguably, in all of English-language literature. Tim, the Cratchits' youngest child, is very ill, and the family cannot afford treatment. With this famous line in mind, Rawle asks:

- What if we modeled our Advent and Christmas comings and goings as if we actually believe that God has already blessed everyone? (*The Redemption of Scrooge*, page 102).

Spend some time discussing this question. In your discussion, keep in mind that not all of God's blessings have come to fruition. Sometimes God's blessings are not realized for many years.

As a group, brainstorm what it could look like if your community lived as though God had already blessed everyone. What would be different, and why? Using the markerboard or a large sheet of paper, record participants' thoughts, and ask:

- How can we make this a reality?

*Optional*: Have participants look up the lyrics of the popular Christmas hymn "Hark! the Herald Angels Sing." You could set out hymnals or songbooks featuring the song or have participants find lyrics on the Internet using their phones or other devices. Have participants read the lyrics closely. Ask:

- How familiar are you with the lyrics to this hymn?
- What did you notice about the lyrics that you hadn't noticed or thought of before?
- How do the lyrics of this song echo Tiny Tim's quote, "God bless Us, Every One"?

Read what Rawle has to say about this hymn on page 102 in *The Redemption of Scrooge*. What is the theological significance of phrases such as, "Peace on earth" and "God and sinners reconciled"?

# THE HOPE OF
# CHRISTMAS FUTURE

## PLANNING THE SESSION

### Session Goals

Through this session's discussion and activities, participants will be encouraged to:

- Consider how our hopes and fears shape our future and how our faith relates to our hopes and fears.
- Examine the role darkness plays in Scripture and in our world today and identify ways we can be God's light amid the darkness.
- Reflect on God's promises for the future and how they affect our lives and attitudes today.

- Explore the idea of redemption and what it means to be redeemed.
- Look forward to God's promised return and the fulfillment of all things.
- Reflect on what it means to "keep Christmas well" and live in Christ's hope for the future.

## Preparation

- Read Chapter 4, "The Hope of Christmas Future," in Matt Rawle's *The Redemption of Scrooge.*
- Read through this Leader Guide session in its entirety to familiarize yourself with the material being covered.
- Read and reflect on the following Scriptures:
  - o 1 Samuel 3:1-10
  - o Psalm 42:1-5
  - o Luke 19:1-9
  - o John 4:4-30
  - o Acts 3:1-10
- You will want to have your DVD player or computer ready to watch the video segment. You might also want to have a markerboard or large sheet of paper available for recording group members' ideas.
- Have a Bible, paper for taking notes, and a pen or pencil available for every participant. You might also want to have colored pencils or markers available if any participants would like to sketch or journal.
- For the opening activity, you will need note cards or slips of paper for each participant.
- If you are doing the activity "Was, Is, and Is Yet to Come," you might want the option of having available hymnals or songbooks that contain "Joy to the World."

## GETTING STARTED

### Opening Activity and Prayer (5 minutes)

As participants arrive, greet them and hand each person a note card or slip of paper. Ask participants to write down three hopes they have for the future and three fears they have about the future. They need not say these aloud. After they've had a few minutes to write and reflect, ask:

- Which do you have stronger feelings about, your hopes or your fears?
- How does your faith figure into your hope for the future?

*God of what is to come, watch over us in the immediate future as we reflect on your promises for the days ahead. Guide our discussions so that we may speak your wisdom and consider how to face the future with hope and faith. In Jesus' name. Amen.*

## LEARNING TOGETHER

### Watch DVD Segment (10 minutes)

### Study and Discussion of Book and DVD (35–40 minutes)

#### Christmas Future

Give each participant a sheet of paper and set out pens, pencils, colored pencils, or markers. Invite each person to illustrate, through drawing or writing, his or her "Christmas future." How does he or she envision future celebrations? Ask participants to consider who might be present at these future Christmases, where these celebrations might take place, what decorations they might expect to see, and so forth.

Allow everyone a few minutes to work, then invite volunteers to share what they've put on paper. (Alternatively, participants could separate into pairs or groups of three and share their work with their partners or group mates.) Then discuss:

- Based on what you've been learning this Advent season, how do you expect your future Christmas celebrations to be different from past celebrations?
- What parts of your Christmas festivities do you expect to stay the same?
- How might your future Christmas celebrations better glorify Christ?

**Was, Is, and Is to Come**

*Read aloud or summarize for the group:*

Christians profess that God was, is, and is to come—that God has been active in the past, is active in the present, and will be active in the future (much like the ghosts in *A Christmas Carol*). It is easy for us to see God's handiwork in the past and present, but what does it mean for God to be active in the future? Ask:

- Read Revelation 1:4. What power does God have over the future? What knowledge does God have of the future?
- What are some things that we know to be true about God's knowledge, love, and power?
- How does God's power and knowledge regarding the future affect our future and our decisions?

- Rawle writes, "A God *who is to come* means that God can be trusted" (*The Redemption of Scrooge, page* 126). What do you think he means by this? What does trust have to do with serving a God who is active in the future?

Discuss how Advent is not only a time to look forward to celebrating Christmas and how Christ came to earth as a human baby but also to look forward to the day when Christ returns in glory.

Read Psalm 98. Ask:

- How does this psalm, which was written long before Christ came to earth the first time, anticipate the day when Christ returns and brings all things to fulfillment?
- How does the promise that Christ will one day return affect how you live your life today?

*Optional*: Invite participants to read the lyrics to the popular Christmas hymn, "Joy to the World." (You can hand out hymnals or songbooks or have participants to look up the lyrics on the Internet using their phones or other devices.) Ask:

- What similarities do you see between the words of Psalm 98 and the lyrics of "Joy to the World"?
- How does "Joy to the World" celebrate both Christ's birth many years ago and Christ's return in the future?

**Redeemed!**

Ask:

- What does it mean to redeem coupons, tickets, or tokens?
- Think about occasions when you've redeemed coupons, tickets, or tokens. Which of these experiences involved redeeming things that you'd worked hard to earn? Which involved things that had been given to you?

Have participants consider two situations in which something is exchanged:

- Earning tickets by playing games at a fair and redeeming these tickets for prizes
- Being given a gift certificate for a meal at a restaurant and redeeming it

Ask:

- Which scenario is like the gospel?

*Read aloud or summarize for the group:*

In the DVD session, Rawle says that receiving God's grace isn't like receiving a discount coupon and using it toward a purchase. A more accurate picture is, God has already offered us salvation, and responding to that gift is where transformation takes place. Salvation has already been offered, and our goal is to respond to God's grace. In other words, we do not have a coupon to present. Jesus is the coupon, and we are what God receives in return.

Read aloud Ephesians 1:4-8, and discuss:

- When a Christian experiences redemption, what is exchanged?
- What does it mean for Scrooge to have been redeemed in *A Christmas Carol*? What was exchanged?

**Light as a Feather**

Ask if participants are familiar with the brain teaser, "Which is heavier, a pound of lead or a pound of feathers?" The answer is neither, because both weigh exactly one pound. It takes only 2.44 cubic inches of lead to weigh only one pound; it takes a much larger volume of feathers.

Scrooge, as a result of his experience and the hope of changing his ways and living a new life, says he feels "light as a feather."

- What comes to mind when you think of feeling "light as a feather"?
- When have you experienced this feeling? What changed in your life to cause it?

Read aloud the following Scriptures, and for each passage discuss the questions that follow:

- Luke 19:1-9
- John 4:4-30
- Acts 3:1-10

For each passage, ask:

- What happened in the person's life to give him or her a light-as-a-feather feeling?
- How did the person change as a result of this experience?
- What impact did he or she have on others as a result of this experience?

*Read aloud or summarize for the group:*

Scrooge, exuberant and with a new, joyful perspective on life, rushes over to his nephew's house. After his life-changing experience with the three ghosts, Scrooge is transformed and accepts not only his nephew's dinner invitation; he also accepts the ghosts' invitation to change his life from one of bitterness to a life of joy. As a result, Dickens tells us that, from that day forward, Scrooge learned to "keep Christmas well." Ask:

- After going through this study, what do you think it means to "keep Christmas well"?

- How has accepting Christ's invitation of grace changed your perspective on your life?

# WRAPPING UP

## Closing Activity and Prayer (5 minutes)

In *A Christmas Carol,* the Ghost of Christmas Yet to Come shows Scrooge what his bleak future will hold if he does not change his attitude, priorities, and treatment of other people. Ask participants to imagine that the Ghost of Christmas Yet to Come visited them. What might the ghost show them and want them to learn? Give participants a few minutes to reflect or journal on this thought.

*Read aloud or summarize for the group:*

Rawle writes, "Christ is born so that God might have ears to hear our wants, eyes to see our need, hands to outstretch on the cross in order to clothe us in his resurrection, and lips to speak the story of good news, that we might share with the world. When Christ's invitation is accepted, we discover that we have been redeemed. We have neither earned it nor do we deserve it. It is a gift from God, calling us to respond in the world with love. Scrooge knocked at the door and asked to be welcomed, and with joy, he was. If Scrooge can be redeemed, then so can we!" (*The Redemption of Scrooge,* page 137). Ask:

- How does this knowledge of Christ's free grace affect your view of the future?

**Closing Prayer**

*God of days yet to come, give us the courage to face the future with hope and without fear. While we cannot know what the future holds, we take comfort in the truth that the future belongs to you and that you will one day bring all things to fulfillment. Empower us, as we head into the future, to be witnesses of the God who was, is, and is to come. We rejoice in your undeserved, but wonderful, invitation to accept your grace. Help us to live in the wonder of this great gift this season and all year long. In the name of the God of past, present, and future we pray. Amen.*

## ADDITIONAL OPTIONS FOR STUDY AND DISCUSSION

### Awkward Silence (10 minutes)

*Read aloud or summarize for the group:*

In *A Christmas Carol,* the Ghost of Christmas Yet to Come is a silent ghost. This ghost responds to Scrooge only by pointing with a finger. The lack of verbal response causes Scrooge to be fearful.

Challenge your group to sit in complete silence for two minutes. During this time, participants should not close their eyes but should keep their heads up and look around the room. Following this quiet time, ask:

- What is it about silence that is awkward and uncomfortable?

- Rawle says of silence, "I have come to realize that silence is what it sounds like when God is listening. It's not that prayers go unanswered; rather the silence is God's invitation for us to continue speaking" (*The Redemption of Scrooge*, pages 120–121). What is your experience of spending quiet time with God? How much of this time is spent listening for God? How much time is spent speaking to God?

*Read aloud 1 Samuel 3:1-10. Discuss:*

- How does the author describe God's activity at the time when Samuel was working under the priest Eli?
- How are fear and uncertainty at play in this Scripture?
- How does God ultimately break the silence?

Give participants time to reflect on their own experiences with God and silence. Discuss:

- When have you felt as though God was silent for an unusually long time?
- How did you react to this silence? How did it affect your relationship with God?
- How did God ultimately break the silence? What did that experience teach you about the silence of God?

**Character Study: Darkness (10 minutes)**

In *The Redemption of Scrooge*, Rawle writes about the fact that darkness is almost like its own character in Jesus' story (see page 113). Discuss:

- What, do you think, does it mean for darkness to be a character in Jesus' story?
- How does darkness pop up throughout Jesus' life? How does it influence events in his life?

- Though we often associate Christmas with light, it is a dark time for many people. For what reasons might Christmas be a time of darkness for someone?
- Read aloud Psalm 42:1-5. Discuss:

  o What do these verses say about darkness in our lives?
  o What do these verses say about how God is present in times of darkness?
  o How do times of darkness affect your relationship with God?
  o What happens to your relationship with God during dark times? (Do you draw closer to God or drift away? How do your conversations with God change?)

We typically think of Christmas as a time of joy and happiness, but for many people it is anything but. Discuss:

- What experiences do you have of Christmases that, for whatever reason, were not merry?
- What is it like to be upset or sad during a season when people are expected to be happy and celebratory?
- How can we, as a group and as a church, minister to those who experience darkness and sadness during the Advent and Christmas seasons?

CPSIA information can be obtained
at www.ICGtesting.com
Printed in the USA
LVOW13s2244161116
513236LV00003B/3/P